MATRIX (1-2)

DAVID MILLER

SPUYTEN DUYVIL
New York City

Acknowledgments:
Some sections of *Matrix (1)* have appeared in *Golden Handcuffs Review*, *Stride* and *Tears in the Fence*.

Matrix (1) & *(2)* was published in two volumes by Guillemot Press (UK) in 2020; an edition that's now out of print.

Library of Congress Control Number: 2024931625

In memory of Dodo, with love

MATRIX (1)

1.

a holy door?
in East London

bread to eat
rain to watch

– weave

robin robin robin
or else starling

....

blue wave
raisins & bread

somewhere not nowhere
by the sea

Virtual Reality
is virtual

2.

bread on table & plate
& rain out the window

a loom in the front
room to the back

&
next to a door

....

I search for food where
there is none

arcade's cafés closed
or else depleted

gulls gulls gulls
or starlings

3.

colours lines strands
green blue red black

or else panels
black yellow & white

– parallel

an entrance into
a different life

....

breadcrumbs oats & raisins
spread on the bird-table

a robin flew down to her hand
graphite & collage oil & beeswax

– arcade in memory or dream

sunlight's brightness
shuttered

4.

"I need to see you" she said
& so we met again & it came into view

that she'd invited friends to her wedding
not telling them who she was marrying

& she'd dressed as a bride
accordingly

& the supposed bridegroom
who was a Catholic priest

was not there
not surprisingly

yet a shock

....

calligraphy entwined with drawing
my words entwined her art

& so we got together
& pledged to marry

O how it unravelled
no wedding no wedding feast

& why was it a surprise & a shock?

fields drained of sea water
white with salt

5.

man becomes boy
becomes bishop

he's enclosed
in scarlet & gold cardboard

he officiates
at three music stands

he recites then intones

energetically he
flaps his cardboard wings

amidst pandemonium
a

language of light
& darkness

....

photograph into drawing into poem
black grey white

she collapsed in the street
– hunger –

& so flee
to another poverty

time? a
narrow

escape

time – time itself
the impossible a necessity

kingfisher gull cormorant heron
sun lake lake sun

6.

cypresses & clear lakes
the brochures said & showed

& so it was
& mountains yes mountains

artworks followed brochures
following photographs or paintings

dumb witnessing
that doesn't & can't speak

....

kingfisher
plunges his beak

splashingly & precisely
framed by two

moments of flight

image image image
poetic & deadly

if you say he writes
then he'll write no more

death has no
favourites

unlike water
– only witnesses

7.

every time you pass
through a doorway

each moment at
or through a doorway

white black black white

we came to the kissing gate
& of course we kissed

dark to bright
a doorway a

book running
water &

feathers feathers feathers
– snare roll after snare roll

lake sun moon stars
in shatters

....

dunnocks splash frenetically
in the bird bath but

the water's now frozen
ice disk thrown into bushes

& now night slow night

no night one said
ever night another

bird bird bird
what the language

isn't asking us
are we now being asked?

8.

no wish to write with a quill
or replicate the colours

the colours non-colours

ink & Chinese brushes
bought in a Chinese supermarket

in Gerrard Street
c. 1973

....

warned by a dream
the white parrot kept to the house

when it was brought outside
a hawk flew down to attack

"peck its leg!" you called
& the parrot did

& the hawk
released it

bitter O bitter joy

9.

famed Filipino artist living in London
– just back from Maoist China c.1972

everything there a spectacle a happening

he accosted me in a Soho bookshop
talking about ancient Chinese poetry

I accompanied him to a health food restaurant
where he added cottage cheese to his soup

....

he stitches
we sew

handkerchief
or hat

or else a shelter
tipi or hut

heavy rain
as I write

not a bead curtain
not a curtain

not beads
not

in dream I held the woman's slit throat together

10.

dripping splattering splashing
running & pouring

rain in patterns
rain on streets windows roofs

rain on water
circles circles circles

houses trams cars
boats ships barges

umbrellas & hats

wind in trees
awash

he filmed
this

he presented a camera
to a dictator

amidst applause

....

information's not to be served
where it scarcely serves at all

– see the mountains move

but many remembered
children so starved they couldn't rise to their feet

not enough rice or other grain

& information was withheld
& lies were told

after the sparrows
dropped dying

from out of the skies

11.

songbirds & goldfish
only distract

keeping them
is discouraged

flowers are a distraction
so destroy them

the owl is a good bird but not
in a cultural revolution

depicting an owl
may be dangerous

so much to ban
so many to persecute

temples monasteries
churches & mosques

vandalised closed
demolished

....

the first emperor
only buried alive

460 scholars

while we buried
4600

hammers nails pliers fists
blows & spit & curses

the first victim a girls' teacher
battered to death by her students

armed in advance with spiked sticks
– sparrows sparrows sparrows

the widower holds up the bloody clothing

where violence reigns
non-violence must speak

12.

will change change nothing?
– awash

unrelenting rain & wind
water in surges breaks over rooftops

black squares or black rectangles
rain & rain & rain

flooding in farmlands & cities
– leap from windows

into rising water
or take to dinghies & rafts

swimming drowning floating
will nothing change change?

windows smashed doors broken
& then walls collapse

will will *change change?*
will *change change change?*

....

variations & trans-
formations

spinning out
spiralling or spreading

heading back
& then out again

swirling soaring
gliding

dark clouds dark sea
piano arpeggios

played quickly
or slowly moving

– the pianist forced to dig hard earth with his fingers
played no more

neither speaking nor hiding of meaning
sign & sign & sign

13.

although
gone

from this
earth

you
said

in the
dream

you'd
come

to visit
me

in
London

(a desolate London
– travelling by bus

lamenting

white pigeons flying up & across
elsewhere

honey oozing into raw earth)

....

loukoumi of course
after moussaka or stifado or loukaniko

beloved squares & streets & alleyways
mostly deserted those evenings

finally sitting at a café drinking retsina
with transvestite streetwalkers passing by

'the world doesn't shrink
it isn't

& yet is'

some are blinded by sun
some by dark

some go out fishing at night
& some drown

his head crushed between rocks

release dove release dove release dove

14.

quiches sandwiches
a large pork pie

savoury tarts

English wedding cake
& another cake (Slovenian)

didgeridoo
& bass clarinet

mandolins
& baglama

clink of ring on glass

....

entering through the door
of a church in East London

& then leaving again

shaded by a white parasol
in the garden of the manse

a bouquet thrown & missed
thrown again & caught

the ring lost in a taxi
found & then lost in the street

& then found again

& then we returned to Bridport
& the kiosks at West Bay

15.

a houseboat
on the Thames

on mud
at low tide

his uncle back in Greece
had built a boat

experimental
in some respect

but I never knew how
nor why his auntie

cried so when we visited

....

he'd crashed an army jeep
driving drunk

& was almost court-martialled
his letters hysterical

& barely intelligible

he & I paused
at the philosopher's door

— he was a bee
keeper

"sign"
he said

& can we speak
for the dead

or the silenced?

in spirit by spirit
signs signs signs

16.

from the ship & the sea
to the port

& back to his rooms
in a downpour

– rest
sleep well

a flame in a
wire cage

lamplight

....

not wetness there
but water

in chains
& released

flow & overflow

– remembering

how she starved herself to death
for the sake of starving children

under Occupation

17.

a symphony whistled
by a philosopher

& sometime architect
an Austrian in England

but my auntie
was a wonderful whistler

(not really my aunt at all
rather a family friend)

no symphonies
no sonatas

no concertos
but O so good

clarity & strength
vibrato & modulation

....

did I want to hit
the wall?

which wall? &
why? I

write & paint & play
music

music might be a
building or

sculpture & then
collapse? or

owls owls owls
?

or goldfinches
in forsythia bushes

18.

seeing reddish-brown
rather than red

& not in anger
a glimpse or a sustained

gaze a gaze
in which

all resolves

a courtyard a gate
a kissing gate?

kissing's
allowed

& applauded

....

& to play
an ocarina

& eat eggs
with leaf salad

tomatoes
& chicken slices

& then play piano
at our wedding

& what did he say
about modal logic?

19.

– remembering how I phoned you one evening
in despair

despair despair despair
spare

30 years later we met again
& soon after we married

so many wasted years
amongst fickle & false friends

along with the few
who truly counted

– in dream
a tiny being sylph-like

wings useless
clogged with mud

stranded in a gutter
crying for help

not me not you
even so

the chines
in darkness

& in wind

....

we are overgrown with information
yes she said

useless in any constructive sense
facts only give reflected light

accidentally creating
clarinet harmonics

as on the zheng
heard in adolescence

but through lip pressure

memory
reconfigured

the intricate interlocking
of two sets of threads

at right angles
a loom in the corner of the room

– her dead love appeared
standing in the doorway

poet musician singer & artist

he was well & smiling
glad to be there again

religion teaches that the soul
can exist when the body disintegrates

now do I understand this? yes
I can imagine many things

& haven't pictures of these things
been painted?

20.

two black squares
two black rectangles

– framed by white painted wood

bus passing window night
Powerscroft Road Hackney night

– manse

– he showed slide after slide
of his art

saying little
until engaged by talk of a friend

sparrowhawks blackjays goldcrests
tawny owls

*...as ornithology
is for the birds*

....

a small house
wildflowers at the door

housebeams from shipwrecks

his poems are to be sung
& only to be sung

knotted in
& knotted

bread cut
wine bottle broken

wine running over rocks

lace flows wild
over rocks

large rock balancing
on larger rock

wind wild through grasses

a cut on the palm
will fester

& delirium begins

earth's end
where the sea

collapses all else

a trumpet call
& a boat returns

with the injured

returns
from a remote island

& the doctor
will go out again

that very night

a glass globe's
dropped & it breaks

final things & present things
to fear & love the sea

no contradiction
no paradox

it's not a sign
it's the wind

the end always now

MATRIX (2)

1.

at
first

light?

moon sun stars no
not any light

.....

a picture
to behold

an image
of what there is

we are here
again

& there
again

white fire
black fire

from which
we return

to dark
or perhaps

never leave

2.

there were no flames there

neither a circle
nor a square nor a triangle

no flame no shape of flames
& no voice

a whisper?
no not a whisper

....

we came to where
the sea had been

or might have been

glacial ingress
& then release

3.

from the window we might watch

we watch
& perhaps there *is*

now a fire out there

we see
& the seeing may heal

the eye
is not on fire

not now
– not always

.....

a bent tree by
the water's edge

maroons
in the distance

explosions
of light

& sound

to signal
& warn

4.

empty ecstasy
a circle winged

fully blank

no

she ran
she ran from this place

& I followed her

in pursuit yes
amongst chapels

....

"let us not pursue"
one said

"yet pursuit there is"
said another

living in a caravan
or living on the streets

& pursuing through chapels
though

the heart
the diamond

rests

5.

& a bird flies up

as I call out
shouting up to the artist

who lacked a doorbell
his studio in Martello Street

mummers in the park
on the way to the pub

– talk of Constable & Turner
inevitably Constable

& so
now in Dorset

an old farmhouse
& converted outbuilding

....

small bird
perched

on the aerial

then flies off
away

caught
in a cold snap

6.

black fire
& white fire

not desire
or at least

not human desire
not

at this first light

....

heavy rain
all night

nonsequences
no

but going back
& forth

I slept little that night
dreaming of friends... dead

who had no desire
to protest or complain

nor to stay

7.

we could
not

could we?
could not forget

all that was is
& might be

forget
the music the poetry

paintings & sculpture
a wave? a smile?

"sentimental" someone said
– emotional yes

....

termites build
so do beavers

& we build too

voles show sympathy
to other voles

& we sometimes do
to others

I touch you
you touch me

in more than sympathy &
thus we build

8.

language is isn't
fire black white

desire? craving? no
desire erases desire

foundational

& the spaces
fulfil & erase

....

I pursue through
the spaces

you said yes you said
& I pursue

in dream

& say

I pursue
you

& yes
& the spaces

in strife

say?

9.

clouds
in blue

light blue

serried

over
us

....

– to feed
the birds

– snow's
on ground

sometimes
ice

bird shit on
the bird table

no bother

10.

green
leaves

flowers

cold
snap

but our eu-
calyptus

survives

....

a church
noted

for its mosaics
outside

the edifice

seafarers
& immigrants

would come
to worship

close to
the centre

of London

& I
noticed it

from the bus
each &

every time

11.

basilica
or chapel

ascension
devotion

not always
a difference

....

there are those
who pray there

& those who sleep
on the pews

when they're allowed
or can get away with it

& some
who do the one

sometimes
& sometimes

the other

12.

yellow | black
grey | black

blue | black
red | black

white | black

owned
ownerless

....

imagination
not

imagination
all

the ocean

the ocean would be?
the ocean would be

13.

"the poor lamb"
she said

her grandson

blood
shit

& light

a glass
of wine

a

lead stack
fallen

– there
were maroons

lights
& the sounds

....

roads
lanes

paths
blind

deaf
& dumb

14.

shale gravel
darkening clouds

slate red sand
rain

reinstated
restored

with the wet-
ness

....

tramping
wandering

silver birches
chapels

green | white
white | white

nothing
& yet something

black | black
black | white

"needs...
we need

to eat
to sleep

to keep warm
in winter

& drink"

15.

star window
morning light

sparrows nesting
in the bell tower

missions churches chapels arcades
in ruins

or else restored

......

fish are multiplied
miraculously

& distributed
& keys given

for the kingdom the

e-
state supernatural

woman's & man's

& these depicted
yes tesserae

16.

yes she'll stop
at alcoves

& the fount

stone steps
up to the bells

– our gate's
rotten

& needs
replacing

– glass rim
& silver ring

always re-
member-

'd

.....

wandering paths
crossing crisscrossing

overlaid curiously

churches birds trees
writing threading through

flowing water waves
we sail on

moiré patterns
nets at night

beacons' light lines
guide & rescue us

17.

glass & shadow
silence & word

I write in red
& write in black

against any reign
I fail to conjure

gladly fail
& the rain does rain

....

a diary of eyes
years slide true

slide false
& nothing prepares

nor unprepares us

thus I am something
compared with something

& I am nothing
compared

with nothing

18.

just outside
the supermarket doors

a wagtail hops
for crumbs & other

leav-
ings

so small
& lively a bird

wind scoops
elsewhere

raised
from rooftops

& elsewhere
orange & blue

openings
in white rock

for doves to come home
& leave again

ghostly

ghost doves
black white grey

....

out in the dark
to feed the birds

peshwari naan

I'll sleep in the morning
& they'll come to feed

dark light light dark

friends
old friends

who come & eat & drink
& leave

19.

each gap between the rocks
in the garden wall

signifies just as well

as a skittish blackbird
hopping across the grass

– signifies
as

a
well

....

what emerges
what intent

or absence

a farewell

to ambitions
so costly

ghostly

20.

into a pit
he goes

thrown by
his companions

& pleasure
is the issue

& the
orientation

– dear dead
friend

you knew

......

I would save
be saved

– all smoke
   – ah my angel

doors close open
close & open

21

deadly confusion
& tangle

thrown thus

ecstasy
no

– ecstatic
in nature

thus gifted

I
now winged

face faces

....

in the garden studio
(a small summerhouse)

in inks
paintings accumulate

black | grey | white
green | green | white

green | yellow | white
black | red | grey | white

– while elsewhere

smoked glass
black

22.

& a wagtail
flies into our house

confused flies
into windows walls

dazed alights
on my hand

& then settles
on a bookshelf

– a power cut
& my wife & I

are left lightless
sitting hand in hand

& then I stumble
through the darkness

for a flashlight

....

black
black grey black

black grey
grey

– nets laid down
for the night

you swim ashore
& then walk....

arched gate
fences

avenues
orangerie

covered mirrors
aviary

23.

"have you ever dreamt
wonderful music

& woke & thought
you'd write it down

in the morning?"
"you'll never do it"

– his descriptions
failed

or rather
he refused

any such
trees & bushes

fluctuating
& so beautiful

gardens &
avenues

oil & wine

oil
wine

......

roses white
Adonis blue

African velvet

a garden-
's

a hospice?
or hospital?

a place for healing
medicinal

curative

or solace
or rest

– did I recognise him?

yes at first
but later I didn't

until he said my name
his face changed

as the garden changed
in fluid light

light dark light

– lightning
you & I

red on the right
blue on the left

thunderclap

lightning again

NOTES

Notes are not really necessary: I merely wish to acknowledge the sources of some brief quotations. Memory is at fault most of the time, and I keep references the way other people keep burrs.

Matrix (1):
Section 5: "a language of light and darkness" is a quotation from Jean (Hans) Arp, cited by John Elderfield in the Introduction to Hugo Ball, *Flight Out of Time: A Dada Diary* (University of California Press, 1996). "...the impossible a necessity": Nicholas of Cusa. (I can't be more specific.)

Section 8: the entire passage beginning "warned by a dream" is a retelling of an account of a dream by a pre-modern Chinese poet which Arthur Waley (re)tells in one of his books on Chinese literature (again, I can't be more specific).

Section 12: for "neither speaking nor hiding of meaning", see Heraclitus, Fragment 93 (Diels).

Section 16: "in chains" comes from Simone Weil, "Straying sea whose waters for ever are in chains", quoted in Jacques Cabaud, *Simone Weil: A Fellowship in Love* (Channel Press, 1964).

Section 19: "despair despair despair / spare": see Gerard Manley Hopkins, 'The Leaden Echo and the Golden Echo'. In the second part of section 19, there are quotations (in italics) from Anni Albers, *Selected Writings on Design*, ed. Brenda Danilowitz (University Press of New England, 2000) and (in an abridged version of the passage) Ludwig Wittgenstein, *Philosophical Investigations*, tr. G E M Anscombe (Blackwell, 1953).

Section 20: "...as ornithology is for the birds" is with reference to Barnett Newman's famous quip to philosopher Susanne K Langer, "Aesthetics is for artists what ornithology is for the birds", subsequently much quoted (e.g. in Thomas B Hess' books on Newman). The second part of section 20 is a homage to Jean Epstein's films set (and made) in Brittany, especially *Finis Terrae* (1928), *Chanson d'Armor* (1935) and *Le Tempestaire* (1947): amongst the greatest films ever, in my view.

When I first began writing *Matrix (1)*, I had a memory of Roy Fisher's poem-sequence of the same title in mind (*Matrix* (Fulcrum Press, 1971)). However, when I re-read Fisher's poem, I realised there was no real relationship at all. I was also aware of John Whitney's three *Matrix* films (1971-72) and Hollis

Frampton's *Matrix [First Dream]* (1977-79), and I probably did learn something from them, but I don't think there is any *direct* relation between these films and my poem.

Matrix (2):

Sections 22-23 draw on Kristin King's *Gardens of Heaven and Earth* (The Swedenborg Society, 2011).

Section 23 also incorporates a brief paraphrase from a conversation between Benny Golson and Horace Silver, in Jean Bach's wonderful film *A Great Day in Harlem* (1995).

If you feel you've recognised a quotation or paraphrase I haven't mentioned, you're most probably right.

I've always thought of this work as unfolding from a single *matrix* in two main complementary manifestations – if that makes sense.